D0687194

Welcome back, kindly sun,

who sent the north wind packing,

in your winter lair you've slept so sound

and rosy-cheeked have woken.

Warm up our earth so corn will grow

and fill the farmer's granary,

warm the wind and waves below

so we can bathe at pleasure.

Welcome back, kindly sun,

bring light to land and water,

to merry song and fiddle tune

we'll dance all night in laughter.

August Strindberg (1849-1912)

I see you in the flowers small

I see you in the sky so blue

Mirrored in streams, and see you too

in lofty trees

in soft green ferns

in bending reeds

in pure white swans

I see you everywhere.

*Rivers meet, each from its own mountain.*

*They grip each other*

*and mix their song and blood.*

*Joined, they carry on stronger,*

*not stumbling as easily against the rocks.*

*No one shall cross us dry-shod again!*

Olav H. Hauge  (1908-1994)

Hamnes, Lofoten

*Every life's a rainbow*
*I saw that clearly today –*
*the good sun and the showers,*
*life's promise in every breath.*

Kjell Sandvik  (1929-1992)

*And oh, how the soothing warmth of the sun*

*like a flood of wellbeing around me runs!*

*And all throughout this balmy day*

*Is the muted, salty tang of the sea!*

Arne Garborg (1851-1924)

*No quieter pleasure there is than this:*

*in summer's fair land*

*to follow the path you've never pursued*

*but all the same can.*

Arne Paasche Aasen  (1901-1978)

*Life is rich loam; fragrance drifts from trees.*
*The sun god stands and turns his burnished face*
*smilingly to our Earth. And lays*
*his vision of eternity over life.*

Jan-Magnus Bruheim  (1914-1988)

Blomberg, Geirangerfjord

Preikestolen / The Pulpit Rock

Stand guard round nature! All foes repel!
Stem those importunate tempers! —
Give the hills leave in the sun to dwell
and let timeless stars caress them! —

Theodor Caspari (1853-1948)

The same sun strove to raise

the sea skywards, drop by drop.

But the way was long

and the water grew homesick,

massed itself in sailing mountains, dispersed into drops

and fell again earthwards

back to the flowers

back to the waves,

borne by the thunder, steered by lightning

and gravity's obedient wings.

Herman Wildenvey (1885-1959)

Kjerag, Lysefjorden

Farthest out at the edge of the morning

light I raised my hands and all

mornings were subsumed

in this one morning

where everything opened to face the Beginning

which lay in

my hands

Kjell Heggelund

Oh God, be thanked for air and light
for the warm south wind and flowers bright.
Be praised for the skerries gleaming there
and for the summer weather fair,
for gulls' eggs and seabirds' mew
for blossoming trees in cheerful hue
for the Earth's new dress when Spring appears,
and for all my life's blessed years!

Alf Larsen (1885-1967)

*Happiness...?*
*It must be those brief moments*
*when nothing has happened — nor is going to.*
*Tiny moments, like islands in the ocean*

*beyond the grey continent of our ordinary days.*
*There, sometimes, you meet your own heart*
*like someone you've never known.*

Hans Børli  (1918-1989)

Can this Earth be so green and wonderful!
And the sky shine so blue and clear!
We stand and marvel. It's hard to believe
that this world can truly be ours...

H. M. Vesaas  (1907-1995)

*Sadly whisper all things here*
*that autumn is near*
*though new-found splendour they possess.*

*Around me I stare*
*and ask: will you ever again appear*
*in summer dress?*

Herman Wildenvey (1885-1959)

*Should I, against all expectations,*
*be blessed*
*and come into the dwellings of the blessed,*
*then I shall tell the archangel:*

*"I have seen something*
*that was whiter than your wings, Gabriel!*

*I have seen bog cotton bloom*
*on the Lomtjenne Bogs*

*back home on earth."*

Hans Børli  (1918-1989)

And this life, I have – ?
I sense faintly, no more,
as through a veil,
I have lived it before.
A brook murmurs briefly,
leaves turn to rust
and soon it is nightfall
and soon we are dust.

Nils Collett Vogt (1864-1937)

*Softer than cotton-grass swaying in the wind*

*deep in the mountain clearing,*

*are the memories that drift through a man's own mind*

*a white-washed, wind-swept evening.*

Olav Aukrust  (1883-1929)

Haukeliseter

such a blue northern sky

the rolling tundra

and the golden plover crying

beyond life

Nils-Aslak Valkeapää (1943-2001)

But each leaf too has a hue all its own:
one of yellow, of blood-red,
of the slumbering clouds and the strident sun,
mauve, indigo lilac – we find it all here.
And side by side, hand in hand go the quick,
the bright with the old and sere,
just as in our world people go side by side,
hand in hand, those who are still young and hopeful
and those who are weary and sinking earthwards.

Sigbjørn Obstfelder (1866-1900)

Jæren

This January sky
is far too cold
light too distant

I live in the hope
that March will be different
the horizon closer

the same bare branches
hold more warmth

there is hope
In looking forward

Sigbjørn Heie

*The sea is so becalmed,*
*the firmament stoops so low*
*with no reflected light,*

*I am sailing into the night*
*of the sleeping ocean below.*

Arnulf Øverland (1889-1968)

Sky and hoar-frost meet
as when two lovers
suddenly meet on the way

*and silver bells ring.*

*No one knows any more who came first.*

Astrid Hjertenæs Andersen (1915-1985)

*Of all the gifts with which we are endowed,*

*none is so rewarding as our capacity for desire, for longing.*

*When we dream, there is nothing we cannot achieve,*

*no door is closed to us.*

Karen Ewald

*On foot*

*I trekked through the solar system,*

*until I found the first thread of my red dress.*

*I am alive to who I am.*

*Somewhere in space my heart is suspended,*

*sparks stream from it, disturbing the air,*

*to other intemperate hearts.*

Edith Södergran (1892-1923)

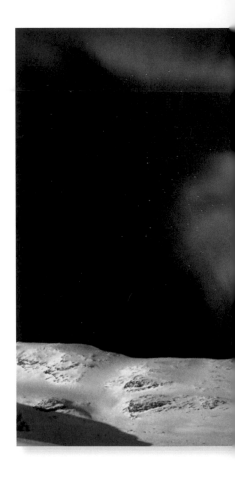

# SEASONS - NEW EDITION 2011

Text and picture selection: Snorre Aske, Jens-Uwe Kumpch
Idea and layout: Natur og Kulturforlaget
English translations, except where attributed below: E. Fraser


**Source references:**

Olav H. Hauge, Dropar i austavind, in: Dikt i samling, Det norske samlaget 1994
                 transl. Olav Grinde

Kjell Sandvik, Hvert liv er en regnbue (excerpt), in: Trosse været, Cappelen 1982

Jan-Magnus Bruheim, Mot mogning, from: På skålvekti, Aschehoug 1947

Herman Wildenvey, Høsttoner (excerpt), in: Mine sangers bok, Gyldendal 1950

Kjell Heggelund, Dagen, in: Samlede dikt, Oktober 1996

Alf Larsen, Kveldsbønn, from: I jordens lys, Oslo 1946

Hans Børli, (p. 22) from: Villfugl, Aschehoug 1947
             (p. 28) from: På harmonikk, Aschehoug 1991, transl. Lovis Muinzer

Halldis Moren Vesaas, from: "Fangar", Aschehoug 1929

Nils-Aslak Valkeapää, Solen, min far, nr. 57, Forlaget DAT 1990
                transl. R. Salisbury, L. Nordstrøm and H. Gaski

Sigbjørn Heie, from: Mørkret set opp fellene sine, Det norske samlaget 1991

Arnulf Øverland, Vår og hav (excerpt), in: Samlede dikt 1911-1940, Aschehoug 1999

Astrid Hjertenæs Andersen, Rimfrost og mild himmel, in: Norske dikt, Gyldendal 1999


**Photographers:** Snorre Aske/www.naturkultur.no, cover + page 6–10–16–24–26–28–30–32–34–38–44
Pål Hermansen/NN/Samfoto, p. 2 + 42, Stig Tronvold/NN/Samfoto, p. 4, Johannes Jensås, p. 8
Husmo-Foto/www.ibl.se, p. 12, Henning Pettersen/www.naturkultur.no, p. 14–18–20–22–40
Nils J. Tollefsen, p. 34, Lasse Jacobsen p. 36, Asle Hjellbrekke/NN/Samfoto p. 46